S0-DZB-908

21st Century Skills INNOVATION LIBRARY

MAKERS
As Innovators

Dash and Dot

CHERRY LAKE PUBLISHING • ANN ARBOR, MICHIGAN

by Kamya Sarma

A Note to Adults: Please review the instructions for the activities in this book before allowing children to do them. Be sure to help them with any activities you do not think they can safely complete on their own.

A Note to Kids: Be sure to ask an adult for help with these activities when you need it. Always put your safety first!

Published in the United States of America by Cherry Lake Publishing
Ann Arbor, Michigan
www.cherrylakepublishing.com

Series Adviser: Kristin Fontichiaro
Photo Credits: Cover and page 1, ©Neil Juggins/Stockimo/Alamy Stock Photo; pages 4, 14, 19, 21, and 24, Kamya Sarma; page 6, Wikimedia/CC BY-SA 2.0; pages 7, 8, 13, 15, 17, 20, 25, 27, and 28, ©Michigan Makers/Regents of the University of Michigan; pages 16 and 23, Pixabay/Public Domain

Library of Congress Cataloging-in-Publication Data has been filed and is available at catalog.loc.gov

Cherry Lake Publishing would like to acknowledge the work of the Partnership for 21st Century Learning. Please visit *www.p21.org* for more information.

Printed in the United States of America
Corporate Graphics

21st Century Skills INNOVATION LIBRARY

Contents

Chapter 1	**Meet Dash and Dot!**	4
Chapter 2	**Playing with Dash and Dot**	11
Chapter 3	**Programming with Dash and Dot**	15
Chapter 4	**What Else Can You Do?**	23
	Glossary	30
	Find Out More	31
	Index	32
	About the Author	32

Chapter 1

Meet Dash and Dot!

Have you ever wished your toys could do more? Wouldn't it be cool if they could move, talk, sing, or dance whenever you wanted them to? If this sounds interesting, you might be interested in Dash and Dot. These toy robots are made by a company called Wonder Workshop. When you first meet Dash and Dot, you can use remote control apps on a tablet

Dash and Dot are toy robots you can program and play with!

Did You Know?

People have been building robot-like devices for thousands of years. Around 350 BCE, a mathematician named Archytas built an artificial pigeon. It was made of wood, powered by steam, and could fly only about 656 feet (200 meters) before it ran out of energy. Robots have come a long way since then!

or phone to play with them. As you get more comfortable, you can start using a **programming language** like Blockly to make your robots do a lot more!

Before we jump in and understand how to use Dash and Dot, let's learn a little about robots. You may already have a favorite movie robot, like the friendly Baymax from *Big Hero 6* or BB-8 from *Star Wars*. Robots in movies often look and behave a lot like people. Sometimes they even have emotions!

In real life, very few robots look or act like human beings. Robots are machines that are designed to do a particular job or follow commands that we give them. They come in all different shapes and sizes. They don't have to breathe, eat, or sleep like people do. That makes it possible for them to do difficult things like exploring the depths of the oceans or the surfaces of distant planets. Robots also work much faster than humans and never feel tired. This makes them very good at factory jobs that people find boring to do,

Scientists and engineers are building robots to be more and more like humans.

such as assembling the same products over and over. They are also used to do things that humans can't, such as moving very heavy materials. Many people use robots to do chores that they don't want to do. For example, a robot called Roomba can vacuum your house for you.

Robots used to be incredibly expensive. Some still are. But today, the electronics and other parts we need to build robots are less expensive than ever before. That means we can have new kinds of robots, like toy robots for kids! Dash and Dot are some of the coolest kid-friendly robots around. They can help you tell

Dash and Dot can be controlled with a tablet or phone to do many amazing things!

stories, put on robot plays, or learn to write **code**. Are you ready to meet them?

Dot is the simpler robot of the two. It is just a turquoise ball with a big electronic eye. It is about the size of a tennis ball. It can roll around, light up, and talk. It knows when you throw or catch it. This makes it easy for Dot to become a part of the games you play with your friends.

Dash is made up of three balls on wheels, plus a head with an eye on top. While Dot can only roll in the direction you push it, Dash can move on its own in many directions. It can also spin, dance, sing, make

Playing with Dash and Dot can be fun for the entire family.

noises, and talk. You can drive Dash around like a car or make it do some really cool tricks!

There's one more thing you will need to get Dash and Dot on the move: a tablet or smartphone. Dash and Dot need something to tell them how to move and what to do. You will use one of several apps to do this.

Wonder Workshop has created five apps for your tablet for use with Dash and Dot. These apps need to be downloaded onto your tablet or phone before you can play with them. You can download them for free at *www.makewonder.com/apps*. The Wonder Workshop Web site also has a list of phones and tablets that work with the apps. Be sure you have at least one device that is on this list.

With each app, you can build a new skill in controlling the robots:

- **Go**—Use this app to connect to a Dash or a Dot for the first time, name it, set its colors, and play with it.
- **Path**—This app gives you four sets of adventures that you can unlock by making Dash follow the path on the screen and by adding actions to the path.
- **Wonder**—This app allows you to build complex chains of instructions that Dash and Dot can follow.
- **Blockly**—Use this app to write code that Dash and Dot can follow.
- **Xylo**—This app is meant to be used with the xylophone attachment. It only works with Dash. Once you have the xylophone and the Xylo app, you can make Dash play music. You can make your own songs, remix the notes of songs from the library of songs, and save your creations to play them later.

You can buy accessories to go along with your Dash and Dot. These are extra attachments that help you make Dash and Dot even cooler. The accessories available include:

- Pieces that attach to Dash's and Dot's "ears" and allow you to add Lego blocks to your robots
- A bulldozer attachment to let you push items across the floor with Dash
- A xylophone to turn Dash into a musician
- A tow hook so Dash can pull things behind it
- Bunny ears and a tail that decorate Dash and Dot for fun

Now that you have seen what Dash and Dot look like and what you need to play with them, let's say hello!

Chapter 2

Playing with Dash and Dot

When you first meet Dash and Dot, you'll probably want to play around a little bit just to see what the robots can do. You may want to start with the Go and Path apps for this.

Go: Figuring Out What Dash and Dot Can Do

The first time you play with Dash and Dot, you will probably use the Go app. This is a simple app that acts like a remote control. The first thing you will need to do is connect your robot or robots to the tablet by getting their **Bluetooth** connections to speak to one another. First, turn on your robot by pressing the power button. Then turn on the Bluetooth signal on your phone or tablet (you can find this in your device's settings). When you open the Go app on the device, it will search for nearby robots and show their names on the screen. You can only connect to one of them at a time with this app. If you are connecting a robot for

Talking to Your Robots

People use words, sounds (like laughter), and signs (like waving) to convey messages to each other. In a similar way, your tablet or phone uses a technology called Bluetooth to talk to Dash and Dot. Bluetooth can connect devices without using the Internet. Many devices use Bluetooth to communicate when they are near each other. Be sure to check Wonder Workshop's page at *www.makewonder.com* to make sure your tablet has the right version of Bluetooth to work with your robots.

the first time, you can choose a name for it and set its **default** color.

You should see a screen with lots of pictures on it. By touching the **icons** on the screen, you can command Dash or Dot to make different sounds. You can even record your own sounds and make Dot repeat them. This app will also let you adjust your robots' lights. You can change the way the lights blink, make patterns, and vary the colors. When you are using this app to play with Dash, you can make it do everything Dot can do. But you can also make Dash move. By dragging the green dot with your finger, you can show Dash how to move. Your finger's path becomes Dash's travel route! It can be a lot of fun to drive Dash around as you avoid obstacles and chase your friends.

Path: Adventures on a Map

Once you have figured out how to control Dash and drive it around, you can set your robots off on adventures with the Path app. This app shows you four different adventure themes. The first one shows you how to draw a line with your finger, add sounds on the path, and make Dash carry out those actions. Then you

Using the Go app is a great way to become familiar with what Dash can do.

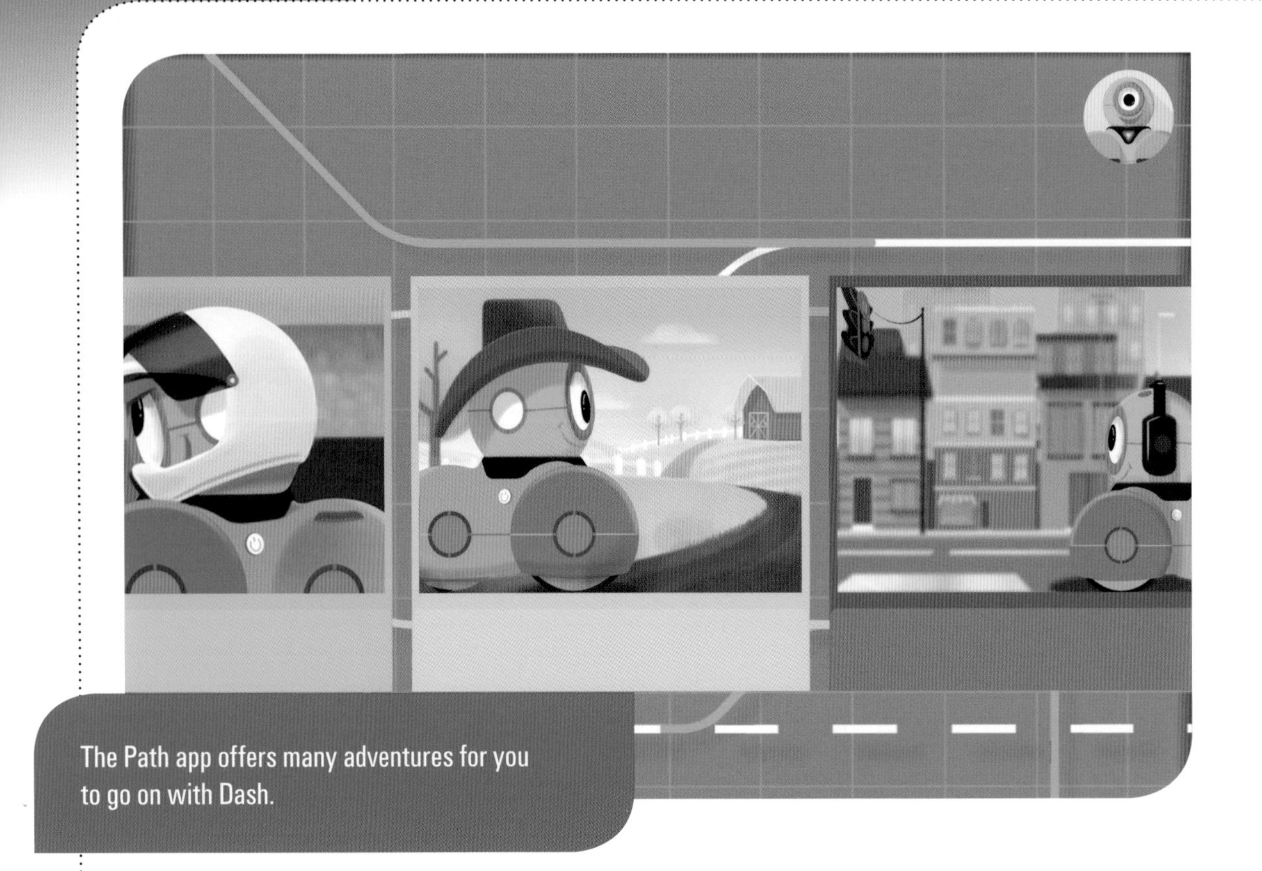

The Path app offers many adventures for you to go on with Dash.

can try your hand at ordering Dash to navigate the racetrack, farm, and city maps. Each map has different levels. Unlocking all four themes in this app lets you create your own adventures!

Path and Go are great beginning apps because they help you learn the variety of things Dash and Dot can do. Now that you're comfortable with using your robots, it's time to learn how to program them.

Chapter 3

Programming with Dash and Dot

Driving Dash and Dot with the Path and Go apps can make them feel more like remote controlled cars than robots. They become more fun when you program them to do things on their own. Programming is the process of giving a computer or machine a set of instructions it can follow. Some people like to use the word *coding* instead of

Keep your friends on their toes by bringing Dash to a party!

Everything you see on the screen of your computer, phone, or tablet is made with code.

programming. This is because programming means creating a series of commands, or code, to tell the robot what to do.

When you become a programmer, you are in charge of making the robots do exactly what you want. Once you understand how programming works, you can learn how bigger and more complex robots are made and controlled. You can also move on to other programming languages that will allow you to create apps, Web sites, and software!

The Wonder app allows you to begin to control Dash and Dot in unique ways.

To program Dash and Dot, you'll need the Wonder app. It is designed for new programmers, so don't worry if this is your first time programming a robot. The Wonder app comes with hundreds of challenges and tutorials to help you learn.

There are a few basic steps to understanding how to use the Wonder app. First, keep in mind that Dash

The World of Programming

How do your teachers tell you what to do? They give you clear instructions that you can follow. For example, your teacher might say, "Open your book," "Go to page three," or "Read the first line." When you are programming, you are the teacher. You tell the computer what it needs to do, step by step. In this case you are using the app on your tablet or phone to tell Dash and Dot what to do.

and Dot can only do one behavior at a time. A behavior is an action such as dancing or changing color. You can link one behavior to another so Dash and Dot can follow each step in **sequence**. But how do you help the robots decide when to do these actions? The cues, or signals, on each link help you do just that. For example, you can tell Dash to use a certain behavior after it hears a clap or after waiting a specific amount of time. Each behavior or cue is shown on-screen as a puzzle-piece-shaped command called a block. When you make a long chain of behaviors and cues, you are creating a simple program.

Once you are familiar with using these tools, you can unlock various challenges in the Wonder app. They have names like "Grouchy Kiwi" and "Curious Sloth." Don't you want to find out what these are?

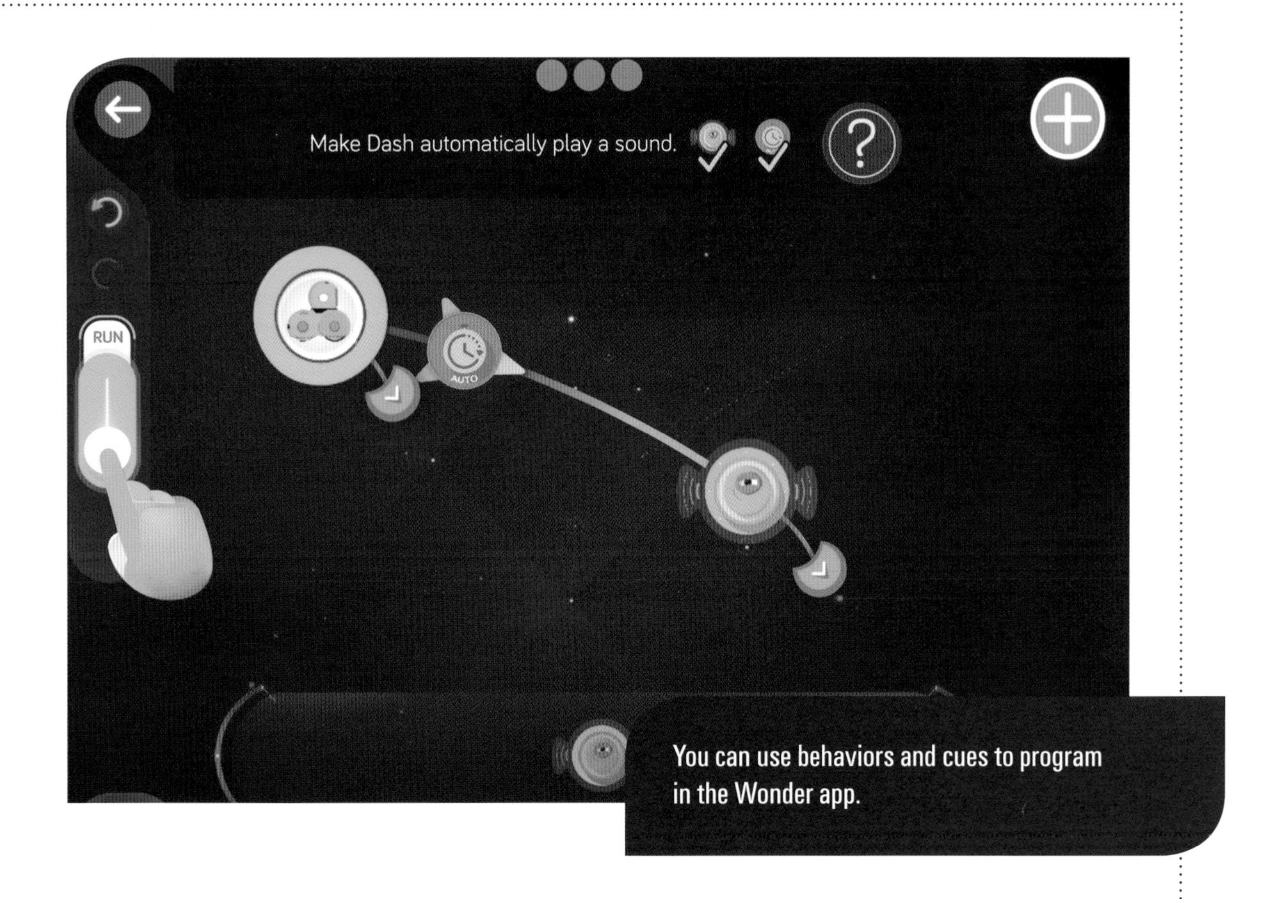

You can use behaviors and cues to program in the Wonder app.

Blockly: Programming on Your Own

Blockly is the most fun and challenging app you can use with Dash and Dot. It allows you to be really creative and solve problems. All the behaviors and cues that you used in the Wonder app exist as different blocks inside the Blockly app.

Blockly is a programming language created by Google. It is a fun way to learn how to code. You can create a program by dragging and dropping different

Make Dash and Dot do what you want with Blockly.

blocks onto the screen and attaching them to one another. The block colors signal what they can do:

- *Purple blocks* help you change the robots' lights.
- *Green blocks* are used for moving Dash.
- *Blue blocks* help you turn the robots' heads.
- *Orange blocks* are for making different sounds.
- *Yellow blocks* help the robots make a choice (such as waiting for two seconds or repeating a behavior three times).

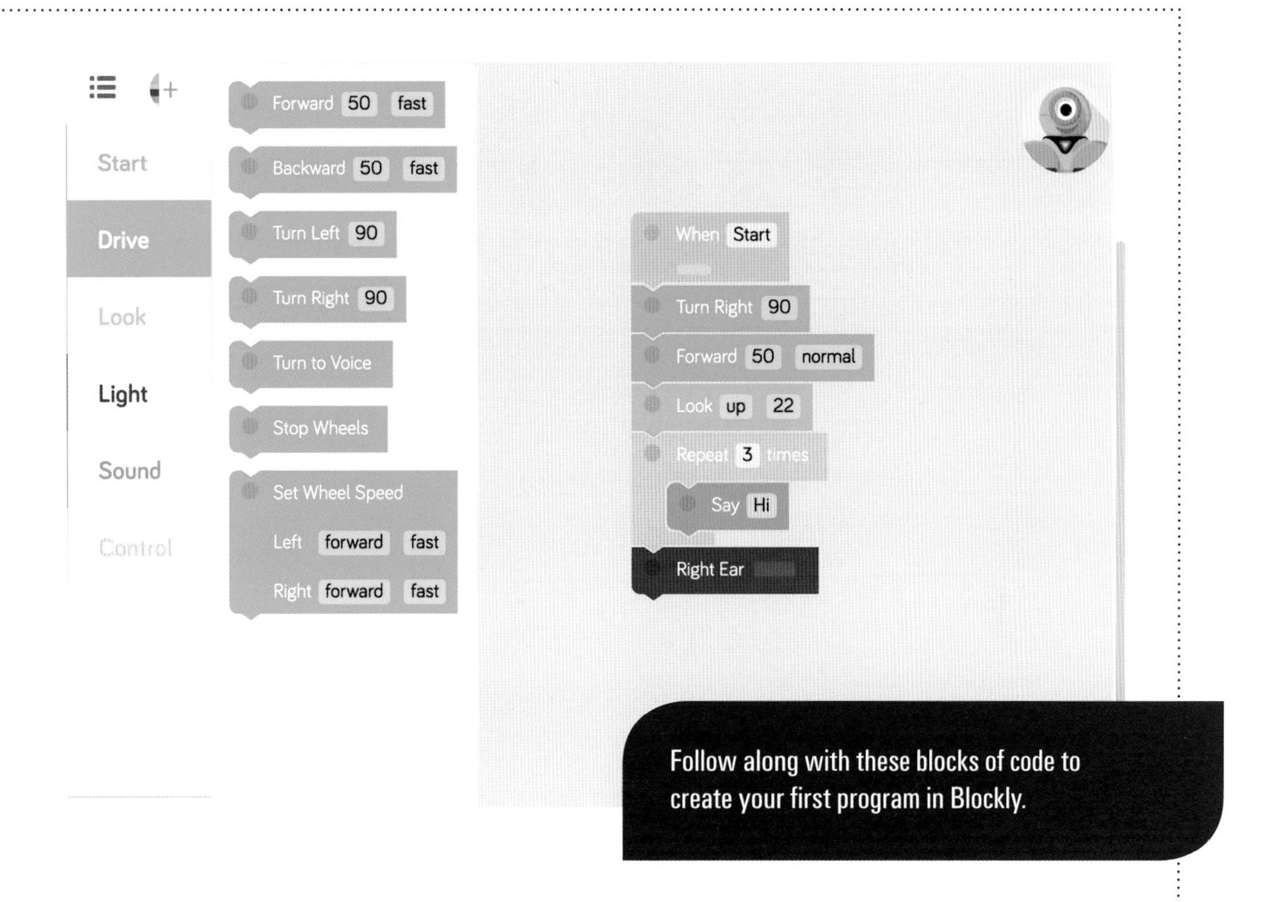

Follow along with these blocks of code to create your first program in Blockly.

With Blockly, you can make Dash and Dot think. In programming, this is called **logic**. This helps the robot decide whether to perform one action or another. For example, you might create a program that tells Dash to check for a certain condition, such as sensing that there is an obstacle ahead. If the condition is met, Dash moves forward. If not, it stays put and flashes its lights.

Let's create a sample program for Dash using one of each type of block. Use the picture shown here to make a similar program on your Blockly app.

When you press the "Drive" option, you will be shown many possible blocks that tell Dash how to move. Choose the one that says "Turn Right 90." Drag it over and attach it under the start block that is already on your screen. Now find out where the remaining blocks are using the colors. Attach them to your program one after another.

Connect the app to Dash and press the "Start" button. Now sit back and watch as Dash follows the program you created.

Take time to explore the different blocks. Pay attention to the changes each one causes. Once you start solving puzzles with Blockly, you're on your way to becoming a programmer.

Chapter 4

What Else Can You Do?

Once you get the hang of programming, you can do all kinds of cool things with Dash and Dot. Here are just a few examples:

Create a Play or Movie!

Your robots can be actors in a movie you create. You can use code to become the director! Using the

Use a tripod to hold a smartphone steady while you make your Dash and Dot film.

Blockly or Wonder app, you can make Dash and Dot perform a sequence of moves. You can make them sing, dance, and say their lines based on cues.

Since Dash and Dot can talk to each other, you can create **dialogue** between them. Remember that good movies feature problems that the characters have to solve. This keeps the story exciting. You can also attach the Lego accessories to the ears of Dash and Dot and build Lego masks and costumes. Create

Wake up, Dot. Let's go on an adventure!

Get your friends together and make a Dash and Dot dance team!

scenery by decorating cardboard boxes with markers, paint, or other art supplies. You can even ask your friends to pitch in. One person can write the script. Another can create the costumes. A third can design the scenery, and a fourth can program the robot actors. What masterpiece will you make?

Go Beyond Blockly!

Once you have mastered Blockly and Dash and Dot, you can start writing code without blocks! This is how professional programmers do their work. Many of the more advanced Blockly games you find online will help you make the switch from using blocks to typing out your own code by hand. With these skills, you'll be able to start learning the same programming languages that pros use to build your favorite video games, apps, and other **software**. Some popular programming languages that Blockly can prepare you for include JavaScript and Python.

Make Your Robots a Part of Your Invention

Once you have solved the puzzles and challenges on the Wonder and Blockly apps, it is time for you to set out on your own adventure. Robots in the real world solve real problems. What problem do you want to solve? Look around you. Dash and Dot can be fun or useful in many everyday situations. You could program Dot to be your bedside companion for when you wake up at night. Or what about a Dash that drives around your house looking for intruders?

Quick and Easy Videos with Stop-Motion Animation

Try using Dash and Dot to create a stop-motion animated movie. Stop-motion animations work just like

What stories will you tell with Dash and Dot?

a flip-book. They are made by taking a lot of photos of an object. The trick is to move the object a tiny amount, take a photo, and then repeat the process over and over. When you play all the photos one after another, it will look like the object is moving! The more photos you take, the more realistic the motion will be. Stop-motion animation can take a little more time than recording a video, but it can be a lot of fun. Movies like *Wallace and Gromit* and *Chicken Run* were made using stop-motion techniques.

Next Steps: Programming

If you really enjoyed programming the robots and making them do complicated movements, you might enjoy learning more coding strategies. Check out the

This robot made with Lego Mindstorms can drive around on the table on its own without falling off.

Blockly Web site (*https://blockly-games.appspot.com*) for more challenges, games, and math puzzles. Scratch is another programming tool similar to Blockly. With Scratch, you can make stories, animate characters on-screen, create your own games, and much more.

Next Steps: Physical Computing

If you want to learn more about how to build your own robot, then tools like Lego Mindstorms might be of interest to you. When you are making robots with Lego pieces, you can create a robot in any shape you want. Once you figure out what is possible with the parts in the kit, you can move on to designing and making your very own robot from scratch. Many schools have FIRST Robotics clubs that use Lego Mindstorms for building robots and entering them into competitions. Find a robotics club near you or start one with your friends!

Who knew playing with robots could be so much fun?

Glossary

Bluetooth (BLOO-tooth) a technology that allows devices to talk to each other without connecting to the Internet

code (KODE) the instructions of a computer program, written in a programming language

default (di-FAWLT) a standard setting that will always take effect unless you change it

dialogue (DYE-uh-lawg) conversation in a play, movie, TV program, or book

icons (EYE-kahnz) simple images or shapes that represent an object or an action in a computer program

logic (LAH-jik) in computer programming, a series of commands that make a robot "think" before acting

programming language (PROH-gram-ing LANG-wij) a set of words, symbols, and rules used to write instructions for a computer to follow

sequence (SEE-kwuhns) the following of one thing after another in a regular or fixed order

Find Out More

BOOKS

Benson, Pete. *Scratch*. Ann Arbor, MI: Cherry Lake Publishing, 2016.

Rearick, Ben. *Blockly*. Ann Arbor, MI: Cherry Lake Publishing, 2018.

WEB SITES

Wonder Workshop

www.makewonder.com
Learn which tablets are compatible with Dash and Dot, find apps to download, and get great ideas.

Wonder Workshop YouTube Channel

www.youtube.com/channel/UCZgluWgYIZ5k5EVHNUziTeQ
See Dash and Dot in action and get ideas for your own robot projects.

Index

accessories, 10, 24

behaviors, 18, 19, 20
Blockly app, 9, 19-22, 24, 26, 29
Bluetooth, 11, 12

code, 9, 16
connection, 9, 11-12
cues, 18, 19, 24

decorations, 10, 24, 25

FIRST Robotics, 29

Go app, 9, 11-12, 14

Lego accessories, 10, 24
Lego Mindstorms, 29

movies, 5, 23-25, 26-28
music, 9, 10

Path app, 9, 13-14
plays, 23-25
problem-solving, 19, 24, 26
programming, 15-18, 19-22, 26, 28-29
programming languages, 5, 16, 26

robots, 5-6, 29

Scratch tool, 29
smartphones, 8-9, 11, 12, 18
sounds, 12, 20
stop-motion animation, 26-28

tablets, 8-9, 11, 12, 18

Web sites, 8, 12, 16, 29
Wonder app, 9, 17, 18, 19, 24
Wonder Workshop company, 4, 8, 12

About the Author

Kamya Sarma is a user experience designer. She has a background in information development and used to be a software developer with SAP Labs.